WARBIRDS OVER WANAKA 2000

WARBIRDS OVER WANAKA

The official record of the 2000 airshow

Ian Brodie

REED

Chris Hinch

This book is dedicated to the memory of
an extraordinary pilot, Mark Hanna.

When a Knight won his spurs,
In the stories of old,
He was gentle and brave,
He was gallant and bold,
With a shield on his arm,
And a lance in his hand,
For God and for valour,
He rode through the land.

Principal Sponsor

Thanks to: the photographers, Prue Wallis, Chris Hinch, Phil Makanna, Antony Hansen, Rob Neil, Geoff Sloan, Ken Chilton and Mark Robson for their amazing images.

Bryan Morton at Computerland, Dunedin for computer support.

All the workers and volunteers of Warbirds over Wanaka for the many hours of hard work put in and Ian Brodie for putting this book together.

Published by Reed Books, a division of Reed Publishing (NZ) Ltd, 39 Rawene Rd, Birkenhead, Auckland. Associated companies, branches and representatives throughout the world.

Established in 1907, Reed Publishing (NZ) Ltd
is New Zealand's largest book publisher, with over 300 titles in print.

For details on all these books visit our website:
www.reed.co.nz

©2000 Alpine Deer Group Limited
The author asserts his moral rights in the work.

ISBN 0 7900 0749 5
First published 2000

Designed by Graeme Leather
Edited by Carolyn Lagahetau

Printed in New Zealand

Front cover photography by Phil Makanna — Hawker Hurricane, Supermarine Spitfire and Polikarpov I-153
Back cover and title page photographs by Phil Makanna

fore Word

Warbirds over Wanaka 2000 was held during the first Easter of the Millennium. It was so special. It was also the 60th Anniversary of the Battle of France and the Battle of Britain, where Hawker Hurricane P3351 flew and fought.

This airshow was by far our most popular one. Over 109,000 people attended over the three days. In 1998 it was estimated that 75,000 people had attended our airshow.

Our special aircraft for the show were the Blériot and the Tummelisa from Sweden, the Hurricane and the Polikarpovs, as well as the two P-40 Kittyhawks.

The attraction for visitors was not just to view the aircraft. It is really a Country Fair, with the enormous variety of attractions available, which included vintage machinery, tractors and the tractor pull, craft stalls and military machinery — a great variety.

Wanaka is such an attractive area to hold this event, with its mountains, lakes and rivers. No wonder many people travel from overseas to Wanaka for this special event. Where else could you combine all this show has to offer?

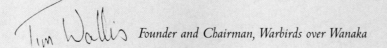 *Founder and Chairman, Warbirds over Wanaka*

Ian Brodie

Jack Stafford, World War II fighter pilot, acquaints himself with Hurricane P3351 at Warbirds over Wanaka 2000. The Hurricane was one of the types of aircraft Jack flew during the war.

intro uction

I was sitting at a bar in Wanaka with an old friend. He said, 'You look worried, Staff.'

'Maybe that's because I am worried,' I said.

'What's your worry?'

'Ian Brodie asked me to do the introduction to the Warbirds over Wanaka 2000 book and I said yes.'

'Well, you don't have a problem, Staff. Nobody reads an introduction so forget the worry. Anyway, you'd talk the leg off an iron pot so just write instead of talking!'

When we got back to Rotorua it was around to the Public Library for me and into the literary section. There I discovered a book of definitions that said: 'The Introduction: an introductory, general, often explanatory, discourse or overview pertinent to a book's subject and tantamount to a preliminary chapter.' I really hope that this turns out to be that, it will be pertinent to the book's subject, for sure.

This book is different to many others in that it could almost be considered a picture book, and people see pictures differently. It depends upon your taste, imagination and the sum of your personal experiences. One man's dreams can mean little to his companions.

Something for everyone is the sum of this book. It reveals the personalities whose support makes the show possible, the devoted engineers who rebuild the vintage aircraft and the pilots who fly them. Finally, it contains some of the most brilliant aircraft photos you could wish for. This biennial publication can be your reference book, your study manual of instruction and your treasured memoir of an unforgettable weekend.

Friday is practice day for the pilots and I always feel it is also machinery day. Several years ago, I walked around these marvellous machines with Jim McCaw for several hours. I couldn't believe the range on display. If you're really in luck you could have a yarn with George Wallis, who has driven and owned almost every tractor I have ever heard of. He is a mine of information and has approached his collection with the same determination and relentless pursuit as his famous brother has to secure his notable aircraft collection.

George and Tim both worked at their father's mill and in the bush. I also worked in the bush when I first returned from the war. My fascination with heavy machinery is shared with both George and Tim. This, together with my devotion to fighter aircraft, gives us lots to talk about.

Wanaka airport at Luggate, changes on the Friday from a quiet country airport to a country fair of a size more like something in Europe. Booths spring up selling an unbelievable range of goods. Food and refreshments are readily available and I always seem to come away with armfuls of flying models for the grandchildren. A day could be spent touring the booths, stalls and tents; take the credit card with you!

As Easter draws near and you move among friends, it is amazing how frequently

Jack Stafford in the cockpit of P3351. Jack trained on Hurricanes in 1943 before joining 486 (NZ) Squadron to fly the Hawker Typhoon and Tempest.

Mark Robson

trip on its own. As I watched the wobbling wheels on takeoff I doubted that it would get off the ground, but get off it did. I thought about all 'those Magnificent Men in their Flying Machines'.

All of this is great but what brings many people to the show are the World War II fighters. The era of the fighter pilot is recreated at Wanaka, and most love this atmosphere. As we watched the Hurricane, the Spitfire, the Mustang and the Kitty-hawk, we were transported back to the violent times when these aircraft battled the Luftwaffe and the Japanese. 'How would I have gone?' That thought must enter the mind of many as they examine the aircraft they have read about. 'How would I have faced battle, would I have fought, would I have won?'

It's comfortable to watch and dream but remember, of all the pilots accepted for airforce training, only ten percent make fighter pilots. Nothing worthwhile is easy. Watch the warbirds and the aerobatic pilots, think of how many times they have tried and failed the manoeuvres they perform so elegantly. Many fully trained fighter pilots never reach this level of perfection. These are the elite, the masters. Many hundreds of hours of tedious training lie behind their excellence.

Admiring crowds are always around the grounded fighters. You constantly hear their comments regarding their beauty and their

the conversation gets around to Warbirds over Wanaka. Everybody seems to want to go or is going. It is not always easy to travel to the bottom of the South Island. It's not always easy to obtain accommodation. It's not even easy, if you start late in the morning, to get a good run to Luggate. Despite all these 'not easys', it's always worthwhile. I've never spoken to anybody

who was disappointed with the airshow. I've never met anyone who didn't find the trip worthwhile. It's something to remember for a lifetime.

This year the vast crowds were entertained by some of the superb skills of some of the world's greatest aerobatic pilots. The topdressers were breathtaking, and to see the Blériot flying above us was worth the

Phil Makanna

glorious lines. People rave about the skill of the designers. How could they produce something of such grace, such beauty?

What must be remembered is that the designers had only one thing in mind. To design a machine that would kill the enemy, efficiently and reliably. A machine that would perform these functions better than all other fighter aircraft, a machine that would give the boy in the cockpit an edge. A machine that would withstand the unbelievable stresses and strains of aerial combat, a machine that could carry heavy and mortal armaments, a flying gun. A murderous raptor designed for slaughter. The bayonet of the sky. These machines were our defence, our protection. They were our fortifications.

That these aircraft turned out to be considered and thought of as beautiful is incidental. Their beauty is in their ability. This inherent attraction was present in the Sopwith Camel. It is still obvious in the F-16. These are the fighters. They can't carry freight, they can't carry passengers and they wouldn't be of much use to a

Warbirds over Wanaka continued the tradition of presenting aircraft that cannot be seen flying anywhere else in the world. People from around the world globe attended the 2000 show this year to see the Russian Polikarpov I-16 and the Polikarpov I-153.

Phil Makanna

Antony Hansen

ABOVE: *Jack and Edith Stafford enjoy their visit to Wanaka.*

OPPOSITE: *Wanaka is an amazing place to have an airshow. The natural amphitheatre created by the Central Otago mountains provides one of the most stunning backdrops in the world.*

Flying Doctor, but in the hands of a well-trained, brave and determined pilot they will repulse an enemy and defend our country!!

Finally, never forget that without the pilot the fighter is a collection of metal parts. His guts and skill are the ultimate need. New Zealand produced such young men in abundance, as we see when we read of Deere, Mackie, Grey, Wells and so on and so on. Remember also the thousands who died. Remember those whose names grace the many memorials erected in their honour. Remember those whose final resting place is still unknown. Please, just say a silent thank you and remember. It is not much to ask, they died for the freedom you enjoy today.

Easter came late this year and with it came the autumn colours. From Queenstown to Wanaka the countryside resembled a top quality calendar. Every brown, every gold, even brilliant red, was portrayed. A dusting of snow on the tops during the weekend completed the postcard effect. On Anzac Day I stood at the cenotaph above the Wanaka township and looked across the beautiful lake to the snow-tipped mountains beyond. Three little spots approached from the north. Gradually they grew and became a Spitfire, a Hurricane and a Polikarpov. Dipping slightly they flew low above us as a piper piped the lament.

What memories filled the hearts of the old soldiers there assembled? The day was cloudless and the autumn sun shone warmly — it was a time to reminisce. The assembly broke up and we wandered down to the hall to enjoy an excellent breakfast in excellent company. A girl sang a nostalgic song relating to the ANZAC occasion. I was drifting into a mood of the past.

I returned to the Wanaka airfield and a flight with Tom Middleton in his Harvard increased the feeling. He recklessly allowed me to fly it and the memories flooded back. I felt the contentment I had at Woodbourne. In the beauty of Wanaka I saw the beauty of Marlborough. We returned to the airfield and I wandered over to Ray Mulqueen's office and hangar. It was getting late; there was no one much around. I looked at the Spitfire and remembered how much fun it was to fly. Sweet and light it seemed to me. I felt it was like a swallow, darting, lifting, diving, at one with the air it lived in.

I looked at that lovely Hurricane, my first single-seater. Solid, dependable, like all the Hawkers it looked brave and aggressive, ready to fight. My eyes settled on the beautiful Mustang. I remembered how it seemed to have more space in the cockpit. I remembered its superb performance. I even remember how it had a tube to piddle into. Bubble hood, superlative vision all round. What a great advantage, like the mighty Tempest, unfortunately not in that assembly.

Using computer-controlled smoke systems, five North American Harvard trainers make sure the visiting public have no doubts about why they are at Wanaka.

The shadows darkened and the mood darkened with them. I could almost feel the presence of past friends. Names came into my mind, never-forgotten names, never-forgotten faces. Did they linger in those shadows? I remembered nights out with them, I remembered the laughter; I remembered the soul-destroying sorrow when they didn't come back. I remembered it as if it were yesterday. Time passes but the sadness remains.

I left the hangar and walked past Ray's office. Someone was sitting at a desk nearby. I let myself out and walked over to Ian Brodie's office. He gave me a drink.

As we left Wanaka on that cool Wednesday morning, I looked at the lightening horizon. I looked at the mountains standing sharp against the morning sky. I drank in all this beauty and blessed my good fortune in being there.

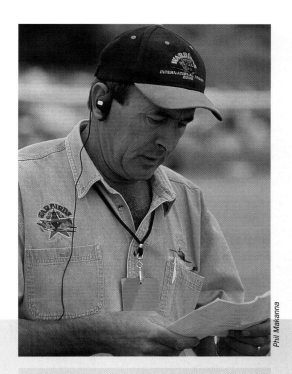

Phil Makanna

Alpine Fighter Collection Chief Engineer/Operations Manager, Ray Mulqueen, looks remarkably calm considering that he holds ultimate responsibility for ensuring all the Alpine aircraft are ready for action over the forthcoming weekend.

Phil Makanna

Now where does this go? Keith Skilling became the first New Zealander to fly a Blériot since 1913, when Swedish owner Mikael Carlsson rated him in the week leading up to Easter.

As our bus made its way over the Crown Range, I thought of the establishment behind the wonderful weekend we had just enjoyed and been involved in. First and foremost the man whose dream started it all and whose dogged persistence and energy continues to build it, Sir Tim Wallis. His brother George, and Gavin Johnston, Ray Mulqueen, all the pilots and all the engineers, Ian Brodie and the museum staff. All those people and many more ran through my mind on that pleasant journey. The 2000 Warbirds over Wanaka has displayed to people from many countries that Wanaka is a world class show run by a truly professional team.

Hell, it's Queenstown airport, this is where we get off.

Jack Stafford
June 2000

Hawker Hurricane P3351

Ian Brodie

In the 60th Anniversary year of the Battle of France and Battle of Britain, it was very appropriate that a veteran from both these conflicts should return to the skies. Hawker Hurricane Mk IIA (P3351/DR393) was shot down over Murmansk in the winter of 1943 and lay in the tundra for almost 50 years. Hawker Restorations, in the United Kingdom, and Air New Zealand Engineering Services in Christchurch, New Zealand, restored her to original condition for the Alpine Fighter Collection. One of the most versatile fighters of World War II, the Hurricane was the first eight-gun monoplane fighter to be produced by Britain and the first fighter to exceed 300 mph. Test-flown on 6 November 1935, it was exceptionally manoeuvrable, with a tight turning radius and excellent gun-aiming stability.

The restoration team are justifiably proud of their work and some travelled especially to Wanaka to look after their baby. One of only eight airworthy examples, P3351 flew alongside the Hurricane of the first allied fighter ace of World War II, 'Cobber' Kain, in 1940. From left to right: Graeme Wilson, Nick Baulf (Hawker Restorations Ltd), Alan Clayton, Owen Pimm, Greg Johnson, Kevin Nicholls, Jeremy Burgess.

Since her arrival at Wanaka in March 2000, P3351 has become the flagship of the Alpine Fighter Collection. On a moody practice day, Keith Skilling formates with Ray Hanna in the Supermarine Mk XVI Spitfire and Air Vice Marshal Cliff Spink in the North American P-51D Mustang.

Manufactured in early 1940, P3351 was flown to France on 1 June of that year to fly with 73 Squadron. Over the next eighteen days she took part in the closing stages of the Battle of France. Her paint-scheme reflects that period of her service.

P3351's under scheme is unique to that time, with one wing painted black and one white, to aid aircraft recognition.

The restoration process on P3351 took over seven years, with companies from around the world contributing parts and expertise. The cockpit is entirely original, down to a 1940 Air Ministry flight computer stored in an original canvas bag.

Rob Neil

P3351

During the escape from France in 1940, a ground crew member was sometimes carried in the single-seat cockpit of the Hurricane (the pilot sitting on his lap). This does not happen in 2000 so Air New Zealand engineers, mindful they can never fly in P3351, did the next best thing. Special baggage was carried during the Sunday afternoon display and then unloaded with due reverence upon her return. Underpants belonging to each engineer had made the flight in their place!

Antony Hansen

Chris Hinch

In a fever akin to an All Black match, Hawker Hurricane P3351 has spawned many souvenirs, from original parts of the aircraft embedded in resin to paintings commemorating her exploits.

ORIGINAL PIECES
OFF HURRICANE
"BOXES"
$50-00

Chris Hinch

Rob Neil

Prue Wallis

In 1941, P3351 was a trainer with 55 Operational Training Unit at Usworth, Tyne & Wear. She was flown by two New Zealand pilots, Pilot Officer William 'Dusty' Miller and Flight Sergeant Ness Polson. In an amazing coincidence 'Dusty' Miller had retired to Wanaka in 1978 and in early 2000 he was reunited with the aircraft he flew so many years ago. In a moving salute to all the pilots that flew her, members of the Warhorses at Wanaka 'G' Flight, accompanied by Dusty and Sir Tim Wallis, escort the Hurricane to the flightline.

Chris Hinch

Resplendent in lemon-squeezer hat, Sir Tim watches as Keith Skilling prepares to commence his display.

Chris Hinch

Prue Wallis

Chris Hinch

ABOVE: *Dusty Miller with Sir Tim Wallis after the commemoration.*

LEFT TOP: *Keith Skilling travels to P3351 on the same type of vehicle that a pilot would have used during World War II — a BSA 350cc ex-Australian Army dispatch bike.*

LEFT: *Hurricane P3351 at rest in front of Sir Tim Wallis's corporate site after a final salute to the man who made the restoration of this aircraft possible.*

Dave Smith

In the dark of the night, a proud warrior rests.

An eagle wings up in heavenward flight
'Til far out of reach of human flight
And gazes on earth from his lordly height
In the clouds of the cold upper air.
And this is the life, exultant he screams
To soar without fear where the lightning gleams
To look down unblenched on sun's gorgeous beams
And be prey to no harrowing care!

Poem by Sergeant J.J. Brimble,
Pilot of Hawker Hurricane P3351.
Killed in action with 73 Squadron, 14 September 1940.

Phil Makanna

Show time looms. The United Scaffolding Team spent a fortnight erecting the 1500 seat Gold Pass stand, and then there was the 1206 square metre marquee to be tackled by Hirequip. Over 60 trade exhibitors displayed their wares to the public this year.

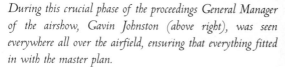

During this crucial phase of the proceedings General Manager of the airshow, Gavin Johnston (above right), was seen everywhere all over the airfield, ensuring that everything fitted in with the master plan.

A sampling of the wide range of trade and display stalls at the show. Items for sale included arts and crafts, clothing, books and jewellery. Also of interest were the Air New Zealand Engineering Services tent, and the New Zealand Fighter Pilots Museum, which stayed open to the public throughout the weekend.

Ken Chilton

Antony Hansen

Chris Hinch

Ken Chilton

Chris Hinch

ABOVE: *Barbara O'Shannessy and Annie Trengrove were responsible for the New Zealand Fighter Pilots Museum tent. They were just two of the enormous number of staff who worked 'behind the scenes' to make Warbirds over Wanaka successful.*

ABOVE RIGHT: *Wanaka resident Chris Riley displays his art in Oamaru stone — a material that can be sawn, filed and sanded to create stunning results.*

RIGHT: *Photographic requirements were in constant demand. Kodak booths placed strategically around the site ensured even the most ardent enthusiast never ran out of supplies.*

FAR RIGHT: *Just one of the many carparks that had filled to capacity by early Saturday afternoon.*

Ken Chilton

Rob Neil

Antony Hansen

The crowd were greeted at Warbirds over Wanaka 2000 with a display from the Central Band of the Royal New Zealand Air Force (RNZAF). It is the largest and only fully symphonic band in the country. The first band made their public debut in 1937, performing throughout the South Pacific during World War II.

To the closing strands of God Defend New Zealand, four A4 Skyhawks screamed into centre-stage to startle the crowd.

Geoff Sloan

Rob Neil

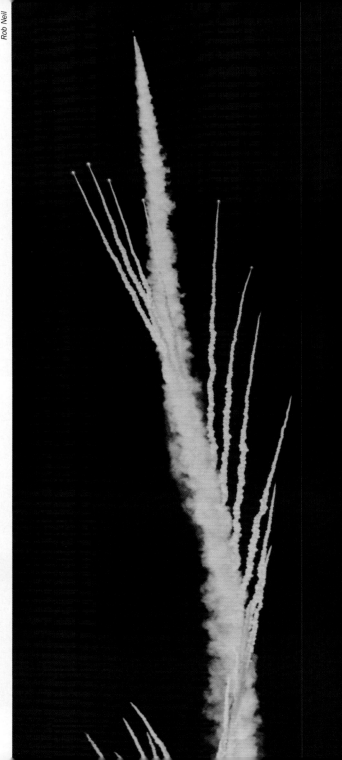

Geoff Sloan

Mark Robson

In service in New Zealand for over 30 years, the Skyhawk is the longest serving combat aircraft the RNZAF has ever owned. In 1981, at an Air Force Day at Whenuapai, the crowd was treated to an A-4 aerobatic team that featured, as part of its repertoire, a low-level 'plugged' barrel roll with two aircraft connected via an air refuelling hose. This was a world-first and has been part of the display ever since.

The dispensing of flares is normally a method of distracting unwanted enemy heat-seeking missiles. At Wanaka, it created a stunning effect for the crowd.

Geoff Sloan

Looks sedate enough — maybe the chicken makes it go fast? Steve Taylor stands proudly in front of his Edge 540, a purpose designed and state of the art aerobatic aircraft.

Smoke and speed — the two elements that combine with pilot skill and talent to make this display fast, furious and fun to watch.

ABOVE: *The wing of this aircraft is built entirely of composite materials and has been statically tested to plus/minus 23G without breaking. Up front is a Lycoming IO-540 engine of 8.75 litres that has been modified to 350 horsepower.*

RIGHT: *The Edge weighs in at only 1200 pounds, and features an amazing roll rate of 420 feet per second. Steve, who has been flying since he was fifteen, has been New Zealand Aerobatic Champion several times.*

BELOW: *Ian Brodie in the commentary bus looking far too relaxed for first thing, must've had his morning tipple to stabilise himself . . . and look at all those buttons!*

Ken Chilton

Over one hundred tractors from around the South Island made the trek to Wanaka. Sometimes taking days to arrive, these enthusiasts are as passionate about tractors as others are about aeroplanes.

Rob Neil

These two 1926 McCormick Deering tractors are owned by Warbirds over Wanaka Committee member, George Wallis. They were found under trees in Central Otago and are still in operating condition. Due to the dry weather in the south, they have degraded little in the last 74 years.

Ken Chilton

The traction engine fascinates people of all ages. A working-scale model Burrell is dwarfed by a McLaren.

Stationary engines were also proudly displayed by their owners. Albert Buckley with his 1914 Associate 6 hp.

Geoff Sloan

ABOVE LEFT: *In 1998, Alby Jordan found this 1890 3½ hp Hornsby-Ackroyd oil engine on the Ironside property on the shores of Lake Wanaka. After two years of work he displays the same item fully restored.*

ABOVE RIGHT: *A working model of a hay press. Children love the small bales but adults are not so sure — the hay is usually liberally spread around cars and motel units on the way home!*

RIGHT: *Bruce Cameron lights his blowlamp in readiness to heat the bulb that will start his 1938 Lanz Bulldog.*

Rob Neil

Rob Neil

Rob Neil

Ian Brodie

Geoff Sloan

ABOVE: *Mikael Carlsson cleans the 90 hp Thulin A rotary engine of the Tummelisa. A rare treat, it is over 70 years since a rotary has been started in New Zealand. This type of engine is quite different as the propeller is bolted firmly to the engine and, along with the cylinders, revolves as a single unit around a stationary crankshaft. The engine has one valve per cylinder and because it has no intake valves its fuel mixture enters the cylinders through circular holes cut in the cylinder walls. Lubrication is provided by castor oil. There is no throttle; switching off the magnetos (an electric generator that provides the spark for ignition in systems that do not have batteries) controls speed.*

LEFT: *The Tummelisa is eased from its container. Owner Mikael Carlsson spent almost ten years rebuilding this replica. He used the original plans, and took measurements from the only original aircraft left in the world, which is displayed at the Swedish Air Force Museum.*

A sea of gold. Spectators in the Gold Pass stand make full use of their complimentary gold caps.

Prue Wallis

Chris Hinch

Geoff Sloan

ABOVE: *Castor oil lubrication can create problems. It is a common misconception that early aviators wore scarves to keep out the cold — the scarves were in fact used to wipe the pilot's goggles clean as the copious amounts of oil were blown back over him.*

ABOVE LEFT: *The Tummeliten (later renamed the Tummelisa) was designed by Henry Kjellson and flew for the first time in June 1920. Used as an advanced trainer by the Swedish Army, it has a top speed of 148 kph and can reach an altitude of 5500 metres. A total of 29 aircraft were produced between 1920 and 1933.*

LEFT: *Big Bird meets Little Bird I. The diminutive size of the Tummelisa is apparent when the Catalina taxies past.*

Phil Makanna

37

Geoff Sloan

Mark Robson

ABOVE: *A rotary powered aircraft can be quite tricky to fly, due to the gyroscopic influence of the rotating engine. Mikael (whose day job is flying Boeing 737s) showed the crowd his aviation expertise, performing loops and rolls in the Tummelisa.*

RIGHT: *The helicopter plays a major role in aviation in New Zealand, whether it is used by a farmer checking outlying paddocks or a rescue service. In all, twelve turbine-powered helicopters from around New Zealand rose out of the Clutha Valley on the Saturday morning, making lots of noise amid masses of smoke.*

Geoff Sloan

Geoff Sloan

Some of the helicopters taking part were (from left to right): two
Bk-117s owned by Otago Helicopters and Richard Peacocke, and
five Bell 206 Jetrangers owned by Brian Beck, Otago Helicopters,
Kitto Helicopters and Peter Garden Helicopters respectively.

One of the early turbine powered helicopters to be used for venison
recovery in New Zealand, this Fairchild Hiller FH1100 is the
only example left flying here. The machine is owned by Goodwin
McNutt and based at Springfield, near Christchurch. Goodwin is
one of the original venison pilots who also started Glacier
Helicopters on the West Coast, a business that services the tourist
industry.

Geoff Sloan

Antony Hansen

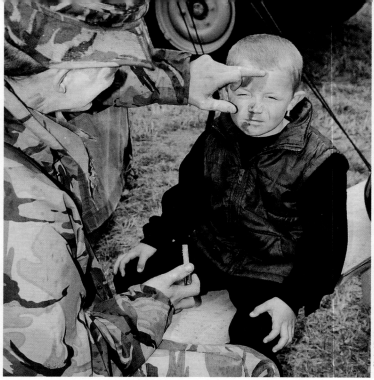

Chris Hinch

ABOVE RIGHT: *The New Zealand Army presented a number of displays to depict their current peace-keeping roles worldwide. Andrew Simpson of Dunedin enjoys a dose of camouflage make-up.*

ABOVE AND BELOW: *Looking much like a camp set up in a war zone, the army gave visitors a sense of scene with armaments, netting and sandbags.*

Ken Chilton

Antony Hansen

An airshow does not happen without planning, planning and more planning. All display pilots must attend the mandatory briefing held every morning. Here, Display Co-ordinator Peter Rhodes addresses the assembled pilots.

Mark Robson

Mark Robson

ABOVE: *The ubiquitous de Havilland DH82 Tiger Moth has been flying in New Zealand for over 60 years. 'CCH' is operated by Wanaka-based Biplane Adventures in Wanaka, who introduce many tourists to the joys of open cockpit flying in a biplane. Popular pilot for this aircraft in the Sunday flypast was Jonathon Skogstad, who has since resigned from Biplane Adventures to fly Cessna aircraft in New Guinea.*

LEFT: *First flown during November 1932, The Beech Model 17 Staggerwing features a backward stagger of its biplane wings to provide the pilot with a good field of vision. Utilised throughout World War II, the Beech features seating for five and has a top speed in excess of 180 mph.*

Geoff Sloan

The Land Transport Safety Authority saw the opportunity to promote their message of wearing seatbelts with an image of pilot Tom Middleton harnessed into a Polikarpov I-153. This sign was strategically placed on the main highway between Wanaka township and the airport.

Phil Makanna

Antony Hansen

Men in Red. Alpine Fighter Collection engineers tow the de Havilland DH83 Fox Moth in readiness for its display. Featuring seating for three passengers, this aircraft spent many years on the West Coast of the South Island, flying with Air Travel Ltd. The Croydon Aircraft Company of Mandeville, near Gore, rebuilt it to original condition.

41

Geoff Sloan

Ken Chilton

This circa-1916 Leyland was used by the Dunedin Fire Brigade for many years. Now owned by Mr and Mrs Nell, they bought her in the 1960s for a 'silly price' at tender.

Ken Chilton

MARLBOROUGH
HISTORICAL
SOCIETY INC.

• BEAVERTOWN   SECRETARY
• FIELD TRIPS   P.O. BOX 308
• MEETINGS   BLENHEIM
• ARCHIVES
• COB COTTAGE
• HISTORICAL MARKERS
NEW MEMBERS WELCOME

She arrived too late for the fire but this 1920s vintage Model T made the trip from Marlborough anyway. Behind is a 1950s Bedford from Balclutha.

Ken Chilton

ABOVE RIGHT: *A 1930s trailer pump, which would have been hooked up behind a truck or the fire chief's car. Behind is a newly restored Ford V8 (nicknamed 'The Boat' because of its shape), which is part of the Dunedin Fire Brigade Restoration Society.*

Ken Chilton

Ken Chilton

ABOVE LEFT: *Rarities — both original and to scale. This 1889 Shand Mason Horse-Drawn Steam Fire Engine was purchased brand new for the Ashburton Volunteer Fire Brigade in the same year. Last used during Ashburton's 1937 Majestic Theatre fire, the machine was placed in storage in an old shed. The old steamer was completely stripped and underwent a total restoration last year. Brigadesman John Newlands painstakingly built the beautiful working scale model from scratch.*

ABOVE RIGHT: *Designed for reaching the top of a burning building, the ladder of a 1967 Merrywether AEC was the perfect spot for Ken Chilton to take photographs.*

LEFT: *The other fire engine display. Volunteer firemen from Wanaka, Luggate and Lake Hawea made up the major part of the emergency team.*

Geoff Sloan

Antony Hansen

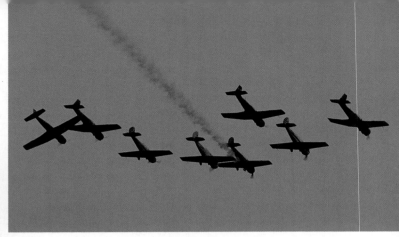

Aircraft and pilots of the Yak/Nanchang flypast (from left to right): Viktor Ostapenko, Sir Kenneth Hayr, Bill Rolfe, Garth Hogan, Dick Veale, Steve Petersen, Jason Hayes and Barry Stott. The Nanchang CJ-6 and Yakovlev Yak-52 both emerged from the Yak-18 design, but here the similarity ends. The Chinese CJ-6 was used as a basic military trainer and is powered by a 285 hp radial engine. The Yak-52 has 360 hp, a shorter straighter wing and different landing gear.

Geoff Sloan

ABOVE: *Air BP is the principal sponsor of Warbirds over Wanaka. In a letter to Warbirds over Wanaka after the show they said, 'Congratulations on yet another very successful event, the show made many people happy and was truly world class.'*

RIGHT CENTRE: *Long time New Zealand Warbirds member Bill Rolfe, in the Rolfe Syndicate Yak-52.*

RIGHT : *Pilot Jason Hayes gets airborne in Nanchang '42' (appropriately registered ZK-WOK). Owned by a twelve-member syndicate and based at Omaka, she is painted to represent an aircraft flown by the Albanian Airforce. Initially operated by the Chinese Peoples Liberation Army Airforce, her new owners are very proud of her reliability and say she operates like a Swiss watch.*

44

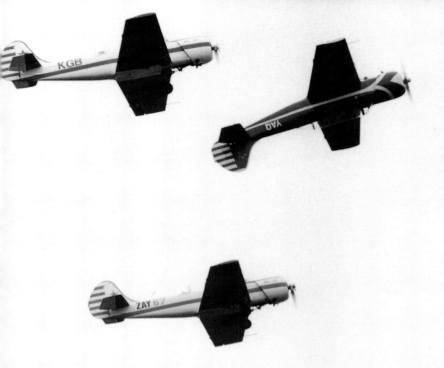

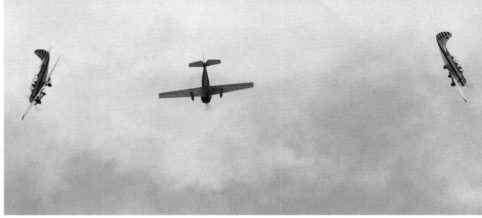

The three-ship formation team, comprising Sir Kenneth Hayr, Garth Hogan and Bill Rolfe, synchronised their display with individual aerobatics from Russian pilot Viktor Ostapenko. Viktor has been with the Flight Research and Aerobatics Group of the Russian Flight Research Institute since 1997, and in the 1980s was involved in the design and flight research programme for the Russian space shuttle 'Buran'.

Alpine Fighter Collection engineers have a perfect lunchtime vantage point from the top of the container that transported the Blériot and Tummelisa from Sweden.

Geoff Sloan

Geo[...]

ABOVE LEFT: *From small beginnings. Warbirds over Wanaka has grown to become one of the largest warbird airshows in the world. This year over 109,000 people came through the gates over three days.*

ABOVE RIGHT: *A visitor from Australia. This beautifully polished Beech Model 18 was built in America in 1949 and was one of twenty aircraft sold for bomber training to the Chinese Nationalist Government for their Airforce after they retreated to Taiwan (Formosa). It later became the personal aircraft of nationalist Chinese leader Chiang Kai-shek. Sold in the 1960s, the aircraft then saw service with the infamous Air America, undertaking covert work for the American CIA in Southeast Asia. Now owned by Australians Tony and Trish Roberts, they especially flew the aircraft across the Tasman Sea to take part in the airshow.*

RIGHT: *The afternoon commentary team. From left to right: Ian Brodie, Jim Hickey, Wayne Parsons and Jeff Watson.*

Antony Hansen

Mark Robson

Geoff Sloan

ABOVE LEFT: *New Zealand Warbirds Association members provide many of the aircraft that take part in the airshow. The Warbirds' Dakota is a popular aircraft, with many people enjoying a ride. The Dakota was the mainstay of New Zealand's National Airways Corporation (NAC) for over 30 years.*

ABOVE RIGHT: *Flying Programmer John Lamont has flown many warbirds both in New Zealand and overseas, including the Spitfire, Mustang, Kittyhawk, Corsair and the Polikarpovs. On-duty, he is an Air New Zealand Boeing 767 captain. Here, John oversees one of the many pilot briefings.*

A conversation between Warbirds over Wanaka General Manager Gavin Johnston and Bill Gordon (airshow volunteer):

Gavin: *Where are you Bill?*
Bill: *Carpark Five.*
Gavin: *We don't have a Carpark Five.*
Bill: *We do now!*

Chris Hinch

Antony Hansen

ABOVE LEFT: *The enthusiastic Catalina Team pose in front of their pride and joy. Arriving in New Zealand in 1994, this example was flown on convoy patrol by the Canadians during World War II. Classified as an amphibian (because it operates from both land and water), the use of retractable stabilising floats were unique innovations of the time.*

ABOVE RIGHT: *Spring-cleaning time. The huge side blisters are a wonderful place from which to watch the world go by. Guns were mounted in this area during wartime, and many U-boats were sunk by tenacious pilots who carried out attacks under some unbelievable conditions.*

LEFT: *The RNZAF operated 56 Catalinas in the Pacific during World War II. ZK-PBY features a typical RNZAF paint scheme from that era.*

Rob Neil

Operated by Nos 5 and 6 Squadron RNZAF in the Pacific, these aircraft rescued 153 men from the sea between May 1943 and the end of the war. The Catalinas also gave escort to ferry flights, dropped food and medical supplies and made ambulance flights. The aircraft earned the nickname 'Dumbo' after the big-eared flying elephant of Disney cartoon fame.

The Warhorses at Wanaka team are an integral part of the airshow. This year they brought their own European village, circa 1944. The Village and Stalag 13 were designed and built by Warhorse members at Bill and Leslie Brittenden's place in Kirwee (near Christchurch), to provide re-enactment opportunities and interaction with the public. The structures took over 2000 person hours to create, using a lot of old timber and unwanted construction materials. Murray Sherer of Dunedin is dressed as a Staff Sergeant, Eighth Army Infantry.

Warhorse liaison person, Graeme Barber of Christchurch, dons a modern headset to explain the team's activities to the crowd from the commentary bus.

WW6213

Ken Chilton

Ken Chilton

Geoff Sloan

ABOVE LEFT: *The many hours restoring these vehicles to original condition are a tribute to the Warhorse members. The Ferret was used as a reconnaissance vehicle to scout around battlefields circa 1950–1970. Manufactured by Daimler (England), it is powered by a Rolls Royce B 60 motor with permanent 4-wheel drive. Its five forward and five reverse gears allow it to go just as fast in either direction. It is owned by Derrick Cullimore from Ashburton.*

ABOVE RIGHT: *Murray Dempster aboard his MUTT (Military Utility Tactical Truck). This vehicle was designed by Ford to replace the Jeep and was manufactured in 1975. It depicts a Vietnam era vehicle, complete with Browning 0.50 calibre machine gun.*

LEFT: *The International Harvester Company in the USA built this half-track in 1943. Originally fitted with four 0.50 calibre Browning machine guns mounted in the back on a revolving turret, its operational role was to follow Infantry advances giving cover against air attack. Powered by a 6-cylinder 450 cubic inch petrol engine, fuel consumption is three and a half miles per gallon with a top speed of 45 mph. This example saw action in France late in World War II and is owned by Peter Lyttle, from Orari in South Canterbury. He bought the vehicle in Denmark in 1997 and shipped it to New Zealand.*

51

ABOVE LEFT: *Stalag 13 allowed visitors to attempt escape from an enemy prison camp. Bringing the scenario to life were guards trying to thwart any such attempt. Arthur Poll of Christchurch keeps a vigil through the fence.*

ABOVE RIGHT: *Clare Oben is guarded over while incarcerated in Stalag 13.*

RIGHT: *Felicity Robinson of Dunedin, about to escape via a tunnel under the potbelly stove. She made it to freedom at the other end of the tunnel, which was carefully hidden in pine trees.*

Ken Chilton

Ken Chilton

Realism is the name of the game whether it be ammunition belts, 0.50 calibre machine guns or 40 mm Bofors guns. The Bofors is an anti-aircraft gun crewed by six people and has a rate of fire of 120 rounds per minute. The gunner is Rod Tempero from Oamaru, and the gun is owned by Bill Mooar from Christchurch.

Chris Hinch

Antony Hansen

It is only when one gets some height that you realise the extent of the crowds at the airshow. Saturday morning at 11.30 a.m. and the crowd continues to grow.

Antony Hansen

Ken

G Flight was an idea developed by Warhorse members to support the Hurricane during set-piece scenarios. Taking scenes from the **Battle of Britain** film, Greg Olsen played Mr Warwick and Leslie Brittenden played Section Officer Harvey. Greg gathered up the uniforms over two years from garage sales, fairs, secondhand shops and collectors. The pre-war experimental webbing is original and was specially designed for the Airforce. The Bedford K truck behind the inspection line at right has been rebuilt and painted in wartime New Zealand colours. A ground crew Battle of Britain truck by Roger Humphries from Nelson also joined the foray.

Geoff Sloan

Antony Hansen

Phil Makanna

Making a guest appearance at Warbirds over Wanaka was Julian Denmead of Mapua, who dressed up as Field Marshal Erwin Rommel, a man respected for his abilities as a soldier and tactician during World War II. Travelling in a 1942 M3A1 Scout car, this picture shows 'Rommel' being driven in a vehicle that was captured from the New Zealand anti-tank Regiment 36 Battery. It is armed with a MG42 machine gun. Above, Rommel stands atop a Scorpion Reconnaissance Tank supplied by the Army Museum in Waiouru in the North Island. It is powered by a Jaguar 4.2 6-cylinder XK petrol engine and is capable of speeds of up to 110 kph.

A 25-pounder (weight of the projectile) gun in action. The standard British field artillery weapon from 1940–1970, the gun weighed two-ton and was accompanied by a Number 27 trailer carrying 32 shells and projectiles. The six gunners were transported in the gun tractor. There are two active gun crews in the South Island, based in Christchurch and Oamaru. Both crews have done a number of public displays and are keen to continue.

Antony Hansen

Mark Robson

To many overseas visitors the idea of topdressing aircraft performing aerobatic routines is quite bizarre. Thirty seconds into the routine by Wanganui Aerowork Display Team and this idea is changed forever. Throughout its 50-year history, Wanganui Aerowork have maintained an interest in formation and display flying and have always supported local aero club airshows.

The Cresco 750 is the first agricultural aircraft specifically designed to accommodate a turboprop engine. It is the descendant of the highly successful Fletcher Fu-24 topdresser, which was originally designed by the Americans in the 1950s as the FD-25 Tree Top Fighter. After a total production of 297 aircraft in New Zealand, the Fletcher was redesigned with a Lycoming LTP 101 engine and then modified again in 1992 to incorporate a PT6-34 turbine. Production of this very successful model continues today.

Geoff Sloan

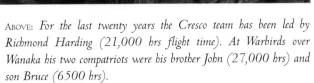

ABOVE: *For the last twenty years the Cresco team has been led by Richmond Harding (21,000 hrs flight time). At Warbirds over Wanaka his two compatriots were his brother John (27,000 hrs) and son Bruce (6500 hrs).*

ABOVE LEFT: *Despite dampening conditions, the huge crowd stayed rivetted to the action.*

LEFT: *The Cresco carries its own movable cloud in a very dramatic example of smoke generated by injecting diesel oil into the turbine engine.*

57

Phil M

By the late 1930s the monoplane was beginning to prove itself as the fighter of the future. Despite this, successes in the Spanish Civil War by the I-15 biplane were seen to vindicate the type in the eyes of some Russian designers, and in mid-1938 the Polikarpov I-153 biplane was test flown in Russia. Based on a restressed version of the I-152 biplane but with the upper gull wing of the I-15, the type featured a rearward retracting undercarriage and a 1000 hp engine. By the late 1940s only two static examples were left in the world. In the early 1990s Sir Tim Wallis commenced discussions regarding the restoration of three wrecks of these chunky biplane fighters and at Warbirds over Wanaka International Airshow 2000 they made their airshow debut. At the same time as restoring the I-153s, the Alpine Fighter Collection initiated the restoration of six Russian Polikarpov I-16 monoplanes. Powered by the same 1000 hp engine, the noise of these aircraft is unbelievable.

Ian Brodie

The 'Chaika' (Seagull) is of mixed construction, with the wings wood with fabric covering, and the fuselage constructed of wire-braced metal tubes and covered with metal skinning forward of the cockpit, and fabric covering aft. Production began in early 1939 and continued until late 1940 with 3437 aircraft built.

The type first saw action in the Far East in the summer of 1939, against the Japanese Army Air Arm on the Manchurian border at Nomonhan. Initially the table was tipped towards the Japanese who were employing their new monoplane fighters, including the Nakajima Ki-26 (Nate), so the Russians introduced the I-16 and I-153. 'Chaika' pilots employed quite a novel strategy in battle. Approaching the enemy with extended undercarriage at about 250 kph, the Japanese assumed they were about to dogfight with an I-15. At the last moment the I-153 pilot would retract his gear and give full throttle — and the tables would be turned.

Geoff Sloan

59

Phil M

To the Russians, these two little fighters are as important as the Spitfire and the Hurricane are to the British. When the Germans invaded Russia in June 1941, the types still represented the major portion of the Russian fighter force. Suffering heavy losses the types were then utilised in the ground attack role and remained in service until late 1943.

Geoff Sloan

Antony Hansen

Antony Hansen

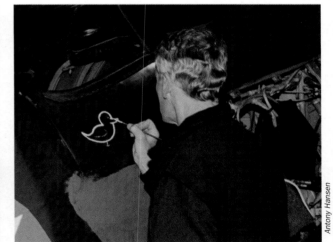

Antony Hansen

Mark Robson

Big Bird meets Little Bird II. Polikarpov pilot John Lanham had the unfortunate experience of collecting a duck in the wing on one of his practice flights. After a safe landing, the I-153 was not only repaired overnight (a tribute to the Alpine engineers and the Croydon Aircraft Company's skills), she was also repainted in a representative Chinese Nationalist Airforce colour scheme. In a scene reminiscent of World War II, Alpine Fighter Collection Technical Administrator, Ewan Fallow, applied one duck 'kill' to the aircraft.

Phil Makanna

First flown in 1933, the I-16 was known to the Russian people as the 'Ishak' ('Little Donkey'). It was the first fighter in the world to go into service combining cantilever monoplane wings with a retractable undercarriage. Blooded in the Spanish Civil War and dubbed the 'Rata' ('Rat') by the Spanish nationalists, the type also saw service with the Chinese Nationalist Airforce in action against the Japanese in the late 1930s. Repainted as P2105/P5360, this scheme is similar to that as flown in 1938 by Chinese Ace, Colonel C.S. Lau.

Phil Makanna

ABOVE LEFT AND RIGHT: *Pilots enjoy flying both of these wonderful warbirds. Stu Goldspink (in '39') touches down and John Peterson ('28') taxies back to the display park. John had only recently converted to the I-16, but quickly came to grips with a 67-year old type.*

LEFT AND BELOW LEFT: *The outbreak of Civil War in Spain during 1934 led to urgent pleas from the Republicans to Russia for fighter aircraft. After a suitable payment in gold, Stalin despatched a large number of I-16's for Republican service. Straight into action, the stubby monoplane mastered most opposition with ease. The I-16 survived in Spain until almost 1950. No. ' 9' was repainted in the markings worn by 3ᵀᴹ Escuadrilla De Moscas based at Albacete (Spain) during 1937.*

BELOW RIGHT: *Stu Goldspink (centre) normally flies Boeing 767s for Britannia Airways in the United Kingdom. He converted to the I-153 the week prior to Easter. He is with Alpine Fighter Collection engineer Geoff Morrison (left) and Alpine Fighter Collection Pilot Training Officer, Tom Middleton.*

63

Antony Hansen

ABOVE: *The debut of the I-16 at Wanaka in 1998 and the I-153 in 2000 should not be underestimated. These types are a significant addition to the world airshow scene. The considerable effort undertaken by Sir Tim Wallis and his staff is vindicated when one is witness to a sight that has not been seen anywhere in the world since the end of World War II.*

LEFT: *A total of eight Polikarpovs — a sight last seen during World War II, and probably never to be repeated.*

Dave Smith

Major supporters of the airshow, the RNZAF delighted the crowd with displays both in the air and on the ground. As Kiwi Blue displayed a precision skydive and landing, Warrant Officer Jack Clayton (RNZAF Recruiting Officer) showed Amy Crawford of Gore the intricacies of an ejector seat.

Antony Hansen

Antony Hansen

Antony Hansen

Geoff Sloan

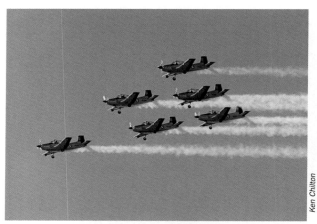

Ken Chilton

Mark Robson

Displaying to the public since 1967, the Red Checkers were led this year by Squadron Leader Andrew Greaves, who is Commanding Officer of the Central Flying School at Ohakea. Flying the CT4/E Airtrainer, the team perform thrilling aerobatics in a type that is poorly suited to the role as it has limited power, which makes station-keeping very difficult in even the best conditions.

Geoff Sloan

Antony Hansen

In use since 1965, the Lockheed Hercules has the ability to fly 92 people to any corner of the world, and then land them on the roughest and shortest of strips. Powered by four Allison T56-A-15 (4910 shaft horsepower) engines, the 'Herc' can cruise at 555 kph with a maximum range of 8843 km.

Rob Neil

Ken Chilton

Mark Robson

Geo

Replacing the ageing Wasp helicopter, the Kaman Seasprite is operated by the Naval Support Flight of 3 Squadron in the anti-submarine and General Fleet Utility role. Capable of day- and night-time search and rescue, its display at Wanaka was truly remarkable, with Lieutenant Commander John Toon showing its surprising manoeuvrability, despite its size. The helicopter has a retractable main gear and is capable of speeds of up to 150 knots. In 2001, the Seasprite will be replaced with the later model SH2G (NZ). Operating off frigates of the Royal New Zealand Navy, the Seasprite also showed its ability to rescue a downed crewmember.

Geoff Sloan

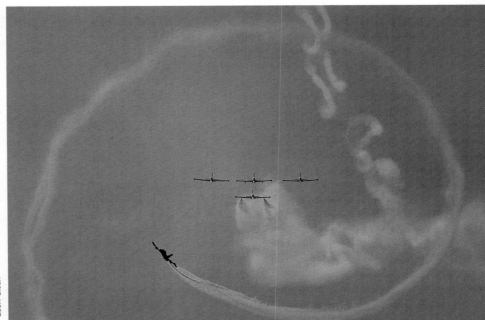

Geoff Sloan

Geoff Sloan

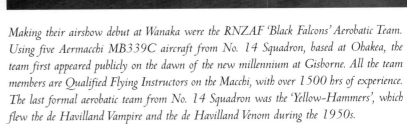

Rob Neil

Making their airshow debut at Wanaka were the RNZAF 'Black Falcons' Aerobatic Team. Using five Aermacchi MB339C aircraft from No. 14 Squadron, based at Ohakea, the team first appeared publicly on the dawn of the new millennium at Gisborne. All the team members are Qualified Flying Instructors on the Macchi, with over 1500 hrs of experience. The last formal aerobatic team from No. 14 Squadron was the 'Yellow-Hammers', which flew the de Havilland Vampire and the de Havilland Venom during the 1950s.

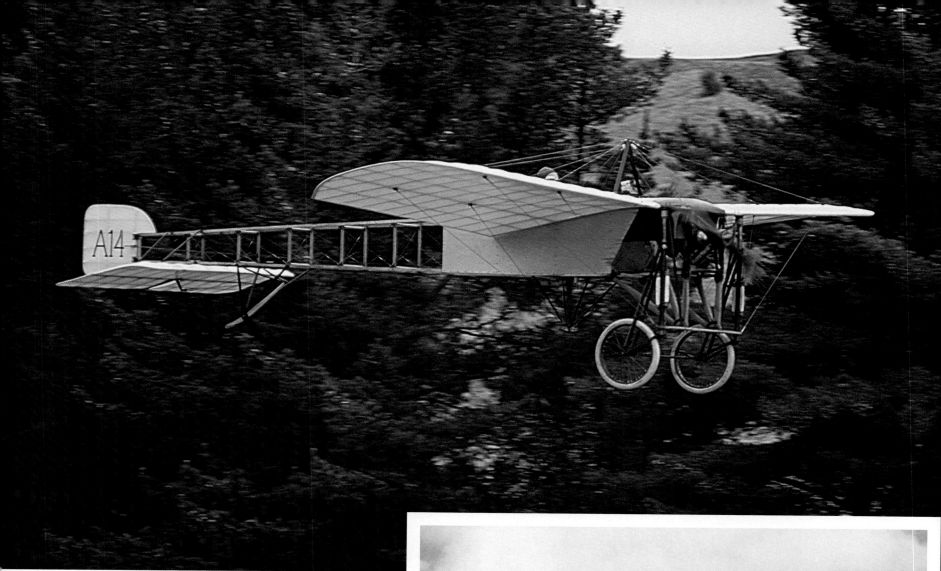

Phil Makanna

What an amazing sight! A Blériot XI returns to New Zealand skies after an absence of almost 90 years. Warbirds over Wanaka imported Mikael Carlsson's original example from Sweden for the airshow. Originally built in 1918, this aircraft was rebuilt in the early 1990s and is one of only three airworthy in the world.

Rue Wallis

Phil Makanna

Of simple wood and fabric construction, the Blériot was assembled and ready to fly within hours of unloading from its container. The Blériot XI is best remembered as the first aircraft to fly across the English Channel. On 25 July 1909, pioneer French aviator Louis Blériot took off from a field near Calais and 36 minutes later landed near Dover Castle. The aircraft saw service at the beginning of World War I but by the early 1920s most of the type had been destroyed.

Antony Hansen

Powered by a 50 hp Gnome Omega Rotary, the Blériot cruises at a sedate 42 knots. In 1999, Carlsson recreated history when he flew the aircraft across the English Channel, 90 years after his predecessor.

Antony Hansen

Ian Brodie

Geoff Sloan

The Blériot also represents a significant part of early New Zealand aviation history. In 1913, an American, Arthur 'Wizard' Stone, arrived in Auckland with his Blériot XI. On 19 April a large crowd at the Auckland Domain witnessed his first flight (albeit brief) when he flew a short distance before undertaking a forced-landing. Not discouraged, he made further flights the same month from Epsom's Alexandra Park (one covering nineteen kilometres). Stone and his Blériot had made the first long, sustained and truly practical flight in New Zealand. On 3 June the aircraft was written off on a fence on the boundary of Napier's racecourse.

One of the more colourful pilots to fly the type was Feilding-born Joseph Hammond. Appointed New Zealand's first official government pilot in late 1913, he flew a Blériot XI-2 (two-seater) that had been presented to the New Zealand government. Dubbed Britannia, it was destined to become our first military aircraft. After several proving flights Hammond was ready to take a passenger. As officials vied for the opportunity, the pilot elected to take a woman member of the Royal Pantomime Company instead. Miss Esme McLalland surely enjoyed the flight but officialdom was not amused. Hammond was sacked and the aircraft was placed in storage and returned to England in January 1915.

Antony Hansen

Phil Makanna

Big camera, little camera or no camera — the crowd are enamoured by this link to the past.

Gunilla Carlsson keeps the Blériot's engine operating at idle.

Prue Wallis

Geoff Sloan

Phil Makanna

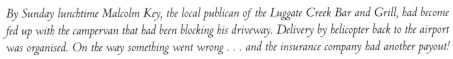

Geoff Sloan

By Sunday lunchtime Malcolm Key, the local publican of the Luggate Creek Bar and Grill, had become fed up with the campervan that had been blocking his driveway. Delivery by helicopter back to the airport was organised. On the way something went wrong . . . and the insurance company had another payout!

Phil Makanna

Antony Hansen

One of the stars of the show, Frazer Briggs and his radio-controlled aircraft. At the age of 24, Frazer is ranked one of the top four radio control aerobatic pilots in the world, after competing at the prestigious Tournament of Champions in Las Vegas last year. His displays on both days were stunningly choreographed pieces flown to music. The crowd stood silently watching the amazing aerobatics, which included hovering the plane like a glider.

73

Geoff Sloan

Geof

Another debut appearance this year was made by the New Zealand Rocketry Association. This 1/7th scale model of a German V-2 was designed and built by their President, Evan More. Taking over a year to build, it has a fibreglass airframe, plywood fins and uses an Aerotech reloadable J415 solid fuel motor. Generating 1280 Newton seconds of thrust, the motor burns for three seconds and then has a seven-second coast time. The booster section is recovered via a five-metre military chute, and the payload via a 1.4 metre chute. The loaded vehicle weighs 10 kg, and the rocket can reach an estimated altitude of 500 metres in ten seconds. This was the rocket's fifth flight.

Geoff Sloan

Geoff Sloan

Ian Brodie

Heroes of the Battle of Britain: the Hurricane and the Spitfire. Built at Castle Bromwich in 1944, Supermarine Mk XVI (TB863) was flown exclusively by No. 453 (Australian) Squadron in the RAF. Utilised in the ground attack role, TB863 continued work post-war as an anti-aircraft co-operation aircraft. Restored in the 1980s in England, she came to New Zealand in 1989 to become the pride of Sir Tim Wallis's burgeoning Alpine Fighter Collection.

Rob Neil

Ray Hanna is one of the most experienced warbird pilots in the world. He has attended every
Warbirds over Wanaka and his Spitfire display this year showed his incredible flying ability.

The Spitfire is surely one of the most well known aircraft ever built. As the numbers of rebuilds continue there are more examples flying now
than since the end of World War II. With final production numbers reaching over 20,000 aircraft, there are now almost 50 airworthy.

John King

A pairing not ever seen before. The Mk XVI Spitfire teams up with a Polikarpov I-153 over the beautiful Central Otago basin.
It is amazing to consider that the Spitfire is the earlier design.

Antony H

Geoff Sloan

Showing the graceful lines of its successor, the Bf-109, the Messerschmitt Bf-108 'Taifun' first flew in 1934, gaining a number of record flights and receiving a number of competition successes at European airshows in the 1930s. Utilised by the Luftwaffe in the communications role, the type featured cabin seating for four. In 1942, production shifted to France and a total of 885 aircraft had been built by war's end. The French continued development of the type after the war with this example, a licence-built Nord owned by Colin Henderson and Maurice Hayes of Auckland. It features a novel gas-operated gun system in the wings, with realistic noise and flashes.

John King

The mighty North American P-51D is probably the finest piston-engined long-range escort fighter ever produced. Initially powered by an Allison engine, the type came into its own after the trial fitting of a Rolls Royce Merlin engine. 'Miss Torque' is jointly owned by Sir Tim Wallis and Brian Hore and is based with Biplane Adventures at Wanaka Airport. Despite being a single seater, modifications made to where the original radio and a fuel tank were fitted have allowed a second seat to be installed and, with the addition of dual controls, one ends up with the ultimate in joy-ride aircraft. Many people from around the world have enjoyed a flight at over 400 mph in the 'Cadillac of the Skies'.

Geoff Sloan

Graeme Bethell and Air Vice Marshal Cliff Spink in the Mustang pair. Cliff, with 1400 hours in the Lightning, commanded RAF Mount Pleasant during the Falklands war and the Tornado F3 Force during the Gulf War. He flies a number of warbirds in England and Europe, including the Spitfire operated by the Battle of Britain Memorial Flight. Graeme has formerly flown RNZAF A4 Skyhawks and Boeing 747s for Cathay Pacific. He owns Mustang NZ2415.

In the closing stages of World War II, camouflage was not considered essential. A number of USAAF Mustangs were left in their bare metal state, giving them an increase in speed of over 10 knots.

Ken Chilton

Easter Sunday — and a special Mustang is flown in for the show. Fooling the crowd initially, it was only when the serial WOW 2002 was seen that the message advertising Warbirds over Wanaka 2002 was revealed. The Alpine Fighter Collection engineers had spent a hurried time that Sunday morning with spraygun and paintbrushes, using a totally removable paint.

Geo

Wanaka normally has 3000 people in its town. Every two years the airshow places a strain on all resources, especially land surrounding the airport. From electrician to restaurateur, all locals play their part in welcoming the huge influx of people. This year accommodation was scarce from Twizel to Roxburgh.

First flown in 1938, the Curtiss Kittyhawk became the first 'modern' fighter to be used by the RNZAF in the Pacific Theatre during World War II. Operating 297 examples, they were responsible for the downing of 99 Japanese aircraft.

Returning to her home base was the ex-Alpine Fighter Collection P-40K, now resplendent in her original Aleutian Island campaign colour scheme. Joining her was Curtiss P-40N #42-104730, restored in Auckland by her owners Garth Hogan and Charles Darby.

To have two P-40s in the air at once was a treat for the crowd and a tribute to all those involved in the respective restorations, both aircraft flying only a few weeks before the show.

LEFT: *This P-40N was operated by 75 and 78 Squadrons (RAAF) in New Guinea between 1943 and mid-1944. The aircraft is painted in its original 75 Squadron markings, which are quite unique as they feature different markings and serial numbers on each side. The reason for this is unknown. Joining this aircraft at Wanaka were her proud new owners and two pilots that had flown her during World War II.*

BELOW: *Taking part in the Aleutian Islands campaign during World War II, this aircraft was recovered from that area in the 1980s and returned to the USA. Purchased by Sir Tim Wallis, her rebuild was completed at Wanaka and she flew as '18', representing an RNZAF example flown by 15 Squadron. Severely damaged in an accident in 1997, she was rebuilt by Pioneer Aircraft Restorations in Auckland and Avtec in Rotorua for her new American owner, Dick Thurman, who flew the P40 from Auckland to attend Warbirds over Wanaka 2000.*

Geoff Sloan

Phil Makanna

Chris Hinch

Geoff Sloan

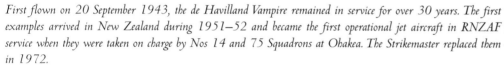

First flown on 20 September 1943, the de Havilland Vampire remained in service for over 30 years. The first examples arrived in New Zealand during 1951–52 and became the first operational jet aircraft in RNZAF service when they were taken on charge by Nos 14 and 75 Squadrons at Ohakea. The Strikemaster replaced them in 1972.

Brett Emeny (NZ5712) and John Currie own the two New Zealand based examples flying at Wanaka. NZ5712 was built in 1958 and served with the Swiss Airforce before being purchased by Brett in 1997. Painted to represent an aircraft flown by 75 Squadron (RNZAF), it is based in New Plymouth. The Royal Australian Airforce flew ZK-VAM before it was imported in 1990 for a New Zealand Warbirds syndicate. It was subsequently sold to John Currie of Christchurch.

Geoff Sloan

With its distinctive V-tail, the Fouga Magister is a perfect example of the growing warbird scene of military jets. First flown in France in 1952, the type went on to become the standard jet trainer for many NATO countries. Retired in the 1980s, the type is capable of speeds of over 400 mph.

Imported by the late Dougal Dallison in 1998 after serving with the French Armee de l'Air, this aircraft's striking colour scheme represents an aircraft flown by the French Aerobatic Team, the Patrouille de France. An Auckland-based syndicate now owns it. The aircraft was flown at the show by New Zealand Warbirds President and syndicate member, Trevor Bland.

Geoff Sloan

Geoff Sloan

Owned by Otago locals Mike Kelly and Murray Paterson, the Mig-15 was displayed by Australian Ray Ekinci. This example was built in Russia in 1958 and served as a fighter until its conversion to the two-seat UTI trainer in 1962. Continuing its flying career with the Polish Airforce until retirement in 1989, she was purchased by Mike and Murray with the intention of operating from Nowra in Australia. Subsequently shipped to New Zealand in 1996, the Mig-15 now lives at Wanaka.

Geoff Sloan

Geoff Sloan

Ken Chilton

Geoff Sloan

Looking all the part like a Japanese Zero, this North American Harvard 'Zero Replica' is very much the actor. Converted to a 'Zero' for the film Tora, Tora, Tora, *she has also appeared in the films* Battle of Midway, War and Remembrance *and* Empire of the Sun. *Flown by Simon Spencer-Bower, the distinctive growl of the Harvard is lost in this conversion, with the addition of a three-bladed prop. Purchased from the Old Flying Machine Company in 1992 by the Alpine Fighter Collection, she has subsequently been sold to an Australian buyer who elected to keep her at Wanaka for the show.*

Proudly proclaimed as the loudest Harvard in New Zealand, No. 7660 served with the South African Airforce until her retirement in late 1996. Purchased by a Christchurch based syndicate she was shipped to New Zealand, where the wings were remounted, and has flown with them ever since. The only non-RNZAF Harvard in New Zealand, she is also the only one to have been imported since World War II. Syndicate member Andy Lyttle formates for a picture.

John King

Geoff Sloan

Antony Hansen

The North American Harvard is a familiar sight to many New Zealanders. Operated by the RNZAF as an advanced trainer for more than three decades, this type is considered the type that began the warbird movement in New Zealand. Retired from active service in the 1970s, the aircraft were sold at very reasonable prices to a number of New Zealand private pilots and formed the basis of the New Zealand Warbirds Association in 1978. Since then, the Warbirds Association has grown to incorporate over 60 aircraft through successful syndication. With its main base at Ardmore Aerodrome in Auckland, and a growing number of branches throughout New Zealand, the association has provided a large number of aircraft for Warbirds over Wanaka since its inception.

The thrilling finale to the flying display at Warbirds over Wanaka is the mock attack. This scenario sees the airfield being attacked by a 'foreign' force, before the defending fighters repulse them. As the fighters scramble from their dispersals the Warhorses valiantly join in the melée, using all their firepower in assistance. This year an enemy rocket base was sited on the far side of the airfield with every effort made to destroy it before the rockets could be launched.

Geoff Sloan

Geoff Sloan

Ker

The V-2 encampment staunchly stood its ground as wave after wave of attack destroyed all the buildings surrounding it. Before long all that stood was the menacing rocket, about to be launched into the Gold Pass area!

Antony Hansen

Dave Smith

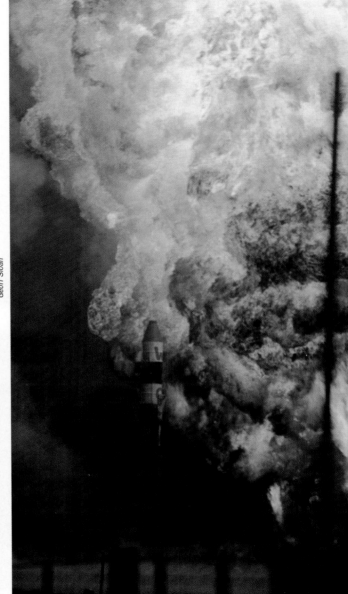

Geoff Sloan

Antony Hansen

Finally a direct hit was made on the camp and the rocket slowly tumbled to the ground, its fuel exploding around the launch technicians.

Kevin (Bomber) Harris is normally the builder and maintenance man for the Alpine Deer Group, but every two years his special talents come to the fore as he gleefully resides over rockets, bombs and explosions. Ably assisted by Peter Gallagher and a team of dedicated volunteers, they provide a spectacular addition to every show. In the Alpine workshop, Kevin carefully assembled the V-2 rocket with a number of 44-gallon drums which airport workers will be looking for over the next two years.

Dave

Antony Hansen

Ken Chilton

Ken Chilton

To the wistful sounds of Vera Lyn, the fighters assemble for one last dramatic flypast in a fitting tribute to the enthusiasm and foresight of Sir Tim Wallis and all those workers and volunteers who present one of the largest warbird airshows in the world.

Antony Hansen

Chris Hinch

General Manager Gavin Johnston (centre) thanks the crowd for their attendance. The aircraft are given one last check before the participants begin celebrations to mark the end of another successful weekend.

Antony Hansen

ABOVE LEFT: *Alpine Fighter Collection pilot, Rex Dovey (left), relaxes with AFC engineers (from left to right) Geoff Morrison, Greg Parker and Malcolm Brown.*

ABOVE RIGHT: *The founder of Warbirds over Wanaka has a passion for aviation that is unsurpassed. The sharing of this enthusiasm has created an event that draws over 100,000 people to a small town in New Zealand.*

BELOW AND LEFT: *The New Zealand Fighter Pilots Museum provides a perfect setting for Sunday night's entertainment as the crowd relaxes to the humour of 'The Blitzkrieg Trio'.*

Antony Hansen

Antony Hansen

Anzac Day

Ian Brodie

Antony Hansen

As Easter ended there was one more important flypast to be undertaken. Anzac Day on Tuesday 25 April 2000 was marked with the flypast of the Hurricane, Spitfire and I-153. As the assembly looked skyward to the passing of these aircraft, they remembered the sacrifices made by the pilots of all nations in their quest for peace.

They shall grow not old. As we that are left grow old
Age shall not weary them, nor the years condemn
At the going down of the sun and in the morning
We will remember them.

Don't forget Warbirds over Wanaka 2002

Easter weekend, 29–30 March 2002